Sauntering with Thoreau

Poems by

Gene G. Bradbury

BookWilde Children's Books Plus

Sauntering with Thoreau
Poems by Gene G. Bradbury
Copyright 2014 by Gene G. Bradbury

ISBN: 978-0-9897585-5-0

Printed in the USA

Book design/prepress: Kate Weisel, weiselcreative.com

Cover photo: The path leading toward Walden Pond from Ralph Waldo Emerson's house.

All inquiries should be addressed to:

BookWilde Children's Books Plus
422 Williamson Rd.
Sequim, WA 98382

www.genegbradbury.com
Writing blog: scribblinglife.com

Dedication

This book is dedicated to my daughter, Hannah Margaret Bradbury, and my son-in-law, Craig Kinney Gring, companions on the road. Unlike HDT they have sauntered far and wide. Like HDT they are curious about and love the natural world.

"We should think sacredly, with devotion.
This is one thing we can do magnanimously."

Henry David Thoreau: Journals
July 27, Tuesday 4 P.M., 1852

Preface

I've walked with Henry David Thoreau for the last thirty years. It seems odd because Henry died in 1862, eighty years before I was born. The other problem is this: it's unlikely he would choose me for company. I talk too much. Henry enjoyed his solitude. He found only a couple of friends he could tolerate on long walks.

This little book assumes our friendship was possible. I have much in common with Henry. And so sauntering through his books and journals I feel I know him. Reading HDT is not for everyone. One has to plow through much in order to find the nuggets that lie in the furrows. It's like hunting for arrowheads. You don't usually find them on the surface.

These poems represent my conversation with HDT. I can't imagine talking in detail about his writing. He wouldn't have tolerated my chattering on. Rather, the poems are my response or reflections from Walden Pond. I sit by the water and drink Henry's thoughts. Some days the water seems bland, on others, sweet and refreshing.

In the morning, a coffee cup in hand, I stop at the book shelf and wake Henry to sit with me. In spite of all his grumbling he seems willing. Maybe fifty or eighty years makes no difference.

The time is greater now because I am older than he was when he left this planet. I will continue to saunter with

Henry and perhaps one day join him among the stars. For now I choose to do as Henry did:

> "It is a record of the mellow and ripe moments that I would keep. I would not preserve the husk of life, but the kernel."
>
> Journals: Dec. 23, 1851

Join me as I saunter with Thoreau through the woods and fields of Massachusetts looking for that one seed pod or observation to carry in my pocket the rest of the day. In this I've found a way to keep his company.

The Author

Contents

Gene G. Bradbury

SAUNTERING

Journal Entry for January 21, 1838

"You will find at Trolhate excellent bread, meat, and wine, provided you bring them with you!"

At Trolhate

On the road
to Trolhate
I'll enjoy
a traveler's meal.

A table I'll set,
meat, bread, and wine
pulled from my pack
in my own good time.

You're welcome to
stop at Trolhate Inn,
eat a meal like mine
if you bring it with you,
meat, bread, and wine.

Journal Entry for June 26, 1840

"He will get the goal first who stands stillest."

Linger Here

Over sandy beaches
messenger gulls
publish daily news.

Sirens wail
in narrow back alleys,
to blend with

children's voices
from skateboard park,
puncture still skies.

I cast my spirit
out to sea, standing
barefoot in wet sand.

Journal Entry for January 12, 1855

"Bless the Lord, O my soul, bless Him for wildness,
for crows that will not alight within gunshot, and bless
Him for hens, too, that croak and cackle in the yard."

Not Mine

Unless I walk the forest
soft as the white-tailed deer,
shape my bed in loam;
fly darkest-night as the
Great White Owl, quiet
over meadow's meal;
and hide in moonlight
like vole or shrew, afraid,
swift to disappear;
I cannot fire the shot
or claim the spirit
to end what isn't mine.

From Biographical Sketch, Miscellanies

"Thank God," he said, "they cannot cut down the clouds."

Holes in the Sky

I stood above the lake
counting tree stumps
where forests stood,
while . . .

rain washes mud
over a broken road
below holes in the sky
and . . .

nature's voice cries,
"Thank God, they cannot
cut down the clouds."

Journal Entry for February 26, 1841

"If I were a physician I would try my patients thus: I would wheel them to a window and let nature feel their pulses."

Point of Land

On a point of land
gulls trace surf lines,
dip, spin, scream
raucous complaint.

Sunlight fades to
bring whispering calm.
Widgeons glide
on gleaming dark water.

Gulls are soon away,
stilling the night.
Nature's pulse slows
into quiet moonlight.

Journal Entry for September 25, 1851

"Some men are excited by the smell of burning powder, but I thought in my dream last night how much saner to be excited by the smell of new bread."

Coming Home to Bread

Stepping along a country lane,
cows lowing, almost dark,
kitchen lights mark the way,
young hikers at end of day.

In the trenches fathers cower,
smoky skies, burning powder,
taste of ashes in warring night,
soldiers raise their heads to see,

in the distance an open door,
mother's shape before the oven,
hope in vain to spread sanity,
warm bread with yellow butter.

Journal Entry for March 25, 1842

"The stars are God's dreams, thoughts remembered in the silence of the night."

Star Leaping

I have not spent time enough
searching the sky for stars,
lying on my back looking
into limb-filtered skies.

My mind has not jumped
from celestial light to light
between darkness so vast,
steps too far from star to star.

It's no wonder I do not know
the dreams or thoughts of God
if I cannot leap into the night,
and trust the darkness
between starry lights,

for I might land gently as a
bee lands on a fragrant flower
and find God-dreams at my feet.

Journal Entry for September 22, 1854

"So live that only the most beautiful wild flowers
will spring up where you have dwelt, harebells,
violets, and blue-eyed grass."

Harebells, Violets, and Blue-eyed Grass

Fill my pockets with harebell seeds,
dream with pleasure of floppy large leaves,
cup-shaped flowers below the sun,
where white-tailed hares used to run.

Line my jacket with violet spore,
sprinkled delicately among weeds poor.
Dainty petals will grow purple and blue
from seed spread wide, the meadow through.

Mix in grain of blue-eyed grass
with its flower cousin, Verna Iris,
and watch the starry petals bloom
awake in morning, asleep at noon.

Holes in my pockets I tramp the land,
spill seeds generously wherever I can,
imagine children who delight and play
among flowers that will grow someday.

What could be prettier, than harebells,
Violets, and blue-eyed grass?

From Miscellanies

"His eye was open to beauty, and his ear to music."

Beauty Passes By

Lithely, she comes,
traveling the road,
her skirts musical
in the wind; dancing
lightly over the hill.
Few see her pass,
basket in hand
covered with lace,
wishing to be asked,

If I had known
where she was from,
what she had seen,
and placed delicately
beneath the lace;
she would have
lifted the cloth for me
to see evening sunsets
hidden there, and
mountain streams
the color of dark hair,
and beauty on the wing.

STEPPING AWAY

Journal Entry for November 4, 1840

"By your few words, show how insufficient would be many words."

Few Words

Voices raise
in hymns of praise,
a charm bracelet of believers.

Outside a trickling brook
winds around blue heron
still, silently praying.

It began in darkness,
quiet creature noises,
praising God without words
in quiet, distant places.

Journal Entry for March 27, 1841

"It is always a short step to peace of mind."

Stepping Away

I wish I had known
the art of stepping away,
visiting a shaman place,
to sit in a cool cave,
peering out into daylight
over valleys below, where
frenzy beats a rhythmic pace,
chaos makes room for fear,
anger follows like a friend.

We become emotional debris
swept daily into dust bins,
scraps of life without peace.

Old age brings time to see
from a cave's opening
into the valleys below,
hear voices dent the sky.
Perhaps it's not too late
when turmoil knocks
to teach our children
when to step away
to find peace of mind.

Journal Entry for December 24, 1841

"I want to go soon and live away by the pond where
I shall hear only the wind whispering among the reeds."

Going Deep

Going Deep

One must travel
into that quiet place,
be covered in silence
like windows in winter snow.

Go deeper still,

where birds no longer sing,
one's breath is all there is,
climbing down, down,
into emptiness, and you
listen with your soul.

Go deeper and deeper,

until a faint ripple
of wonder waits
like a beautiful gem
to be unearthed,
pocketed in silence.

From this deep place,

peace is carried up,
all becomes clear,
snow melts,
birds sing,
you live again.

Journal Entry for December 29, 1841

"These motions everywhere in Nature must surely be the circulations of God; . . . the running stream, the waving tree, the roving wind, whence else their infinite health and freedom."

Job Listened

Job did the right thing
when push came to shove:
he listened to the voices.
"Where were you, Job?"
"Where were you when
the foundations were laid?"
Job may not have liked it,
but he listened to the wind
as Yahweh's voice echoed,
whirling around him like
a tornado ripping the roof
off the house, empty, now.
His head began to swim,
buzzing out of control.
Job caught up in voices,
his ears pounding, hears
running streams, waving trees,
roving winds, flying debris.
Amidst the vortex of words
Job listened. What could he do,
face to face
with the circulations of God?

Journal Entry for July 7, 1851

"I believe that the mind can be profaned by the habit of
attending to trivial things, so that all our thoughts shall be
tinged with triviality. They shall be dusty as the stones in
the street."

Beyond Triviality

Sometimes, alone at night,
I feel falling all around
dust particles in the dark.

Wish instead for snowflakes
cold and pure in my hair.
I lift my eyes to embrace
a thought sent from afar.

You said, "Listen to the night,
hope comes from the stars."

Journal Entry for June 4, 1852

"Ah, those mornings when you are awakened by the
singing, the matins of the birds!"

Matins

I hear the gathered chorus,
practice about to begin,
singers robed in morning glory.

Their stern conductor, anxious
baton raised in feathered wing,
demands avian quiet, please.

Stilled, I sip my coffee,
hear the notes of blessing
from the ever singing trees.

Journal Entry for June 15, 1852 at 8:00 p.m.

"It is candlelight. The first fishes leap. The meadows sparkle with the coppery light of fire-flies."

Concord Night

Candles in the window
flicker, teasing moth wings.
Rocking chairs on the porch
begin their creaking song,
joined by a cricket band.
On the creek a quick-dimpled
splash of fish in moonlight
sends fire-flies, blinking.

The paling light quivers,
dances on meadow lakes,
leaps off mountain snow.
Hours pass, candles burn low,
fire-flies dream,
rocking chairs grow quiet,
in bed sleepers listen
to noises in the night.

The cricket band plays on.

Journal Entry for November 3, 1853

"No other creature effects such changes in nature as man."

Lament

It's gone now, like a quarter
in a magician's handkerchief,
demolished like T.E. Scott's* house
by order of the Town Council.

Lost like the keys searched for,
not where they're supposed to be.
The young boy's picture changed
into an old man's photograph.

Where is the track of pasture,
woodland orchard and swamp,
marked by the Carlisle Road,
where Henry saw blue laurel buds?

Does Thoreau still wander there,
standing in Mason's Pasture,
smelling pitch pine
as he did long ago?

*Early pioneer of Tescott, Kansas

Journal Entry for March 11, 1856

"The man is richest whose pleasures are the cheapest."

The Resident

In the Carlyle Hotel
his room allows
muffled hall noises.
He turns to Thoreau
before a morning fire.

Taking his book
he rides number one
to resident dining,
breakfasts quietly,
eggs with ham.

It's Monday's pleasure,
the flap of kitchen doors,
rustle of today's paper,
clink of cups and saucers,
a gray-haired lady sneezes.

He folds his napkin,
beside a Spode china plate,
returns to his room alone,
happy, to be out of touch
with the world.

Journal Entry for June 28, 1840

"The profane never hear music, the holy ever hear it."

The Aspen Grove

A young boy died I knew well
in the fall of a certain year.
I went alone to the aspen grove,
where trees drop paper tears.

Surrounded by aspen breath,
forest voices prayed,
let grief fall like my leaves
healing is on its way.

Comfort came as whispers,
wind-born from aspen limbs,
softly like a cathedral choir,
covering grief within.

"Do not move," my body said,
"Listen to these dying things.
Remember him, whom you loved,
these trees will bloom again."

Journal Entry for November 2, 1840

"The soul does not inspect but behold. Like the lily, or the crystal or the rock, it looks in the face of the sky."

Trying Too Hard

Today I'll be a lily
face to the sky
petals open,
kissed by bees
simply a lily,
not complex me.

Tomorrow a crystal
that's what I'll be
letting sunlight
dance through eyes,
simply a crystal,
untroubled me.

I'll be a rock,
absorb warm sun,
on a mountain
where lizards run
simply a rock,
and,

when others pass
I'll be very still,
lily, crystal, rock
hear them say,
I'd like to be a lily,
someday.

LET THE CHILD IN ME DELIGHT

Journal Entry for August 18, 1841

"In the morning the crickets snore, in the afternoon they chirp; at midnight they dream."

When Crickets Snore

How it must sound
when crickets snore
under dew-wet grass
in dawn-tallow light.

How they must sleep,
legs dangled, hanging,
sprawled in their beds,
in cricket pajamas.

Do they snore
loud cricket thunder
or soft and light like
wind ruffled leaves?

Do spider webs shake
and ant hills tremble
when all of the crickets
snore village snores?

By cricket watch
from noon beds tumble,
part curtains of grass
and begin cricket talk.

How it must feel
to spring into sky,
see the whole world
with bright cricket eyes?

At midnight, when
grasses are cooling,
a sliver ear moon
listens to hear. . .

first one, then many
thousands of crickets
dancing in shadows,
long limbs snapping.

At last, to soft rooms,
step all cricket children
to put on pajamas
and fold cricket clothes.

Lying in grass beds,
spindly legs hanging
sprawled in the night,
crickets are dreaming?

How it must sound
to hear crickets sleeping
in dew-wet grass
as night winds blow.

Journal Entry for December 29, 1841

"I can see nothing so proper and holy as unrelaxed play and frolic in this bower God has built for us."

Child's Play

Holding her giggle
among laughing lilac leaves.
Unseen by prying eyes.

Her thoughts flow
in the veins of leaves
imaginary dreams,
in a bower so holy.

She whispers to her friend,
Alaska Flower Fountain,
secrets
in the house God built.

Journal Entry for March 26, 1842

"I wish to communicate those parts of my life
which I would gladly live again."

White Comfort

Gray hands pull white silence
over the freckled face of earth.
White muslin hides debris.
All is fresh. All is bright.

In a brief snow-fall morning
a pure moment out of time,
I know . . .
I would come again tomorrow
to walk in new falling snow.

Journal Entry for December 25, 1851

"If there is not something mystical in your explanation, something unexplainable to the understanding, some elements of mystery, it is quite insufficient."

Imagination

See that star. Does it know me?
Who's to tell me it isn't so?
You say, "The earth is spinning,
all the world is mystical."

Don't tell me leaves aren't ships
or circus clowns don't really fly.
Dogs do like peppermint, I know
leaves are questions floating by.

My dreams are whirling planets,
elephants come from a crayon box,
trees talk, gray horses listen,
nothing here is orthodox.

Come, sweep stardust in a pan,
packaged, sent to friends you know
who have no imagination,
no room for starlight afterglow.

Journal Entry for December 27, 1851

"The man is blessed who everyday is permitted to behold anything so pure and serene as the western sky at sunset, while revolutions vex the world."

Let the Child in Me Delight

All is still but a swirling tide.
Gazing west over Angeles Bay
sunlight fades, stepping slowly,
sleepy child on her way.

Orange pajamas flash before me
off to sleep far below,
clouds catch her kiss goodnight
she waves a fading twilight glow.

A silent child gone to sea,
we're left alone in winter's light,
slightly orange, slightly red,
all is still, all is night.

Journal Entry for June 9, 1852

"Ah, that I were so much a child that I could unfailingly draw music from a quart pot."

The Pot's Drawer

She knew where to go.
Three year olds always know.
Get there anyway you can.
In the bottom drawer
near grandma's stove.
You won't find a doll,
Pooh Bear, or Tigger either.
It's pots and pans that bang,
lids that sound like cow bells.
It's music delight and noise
where three-year-old hands
make music from a quart pot.

Journal Entry for June 24, 1852 at 8:30 p.m.

"The great story at night is the moon's adventures with the clouds. What innumerable encounters she has had with them!"

Moon Games

Twas a windy night,
leaves frolicked in air
clouds danced over earth
in moonlight fare.

In celestial games
clouds played hide and seek.
The moon stood still
over children asleep.

So passed midnight hours
clouds sporting with moon,
and down on the earth
crickets sang cricket tunes.

Journal Entry for June 2, 1853

"When I awake I hear the low, universal chirping
or twittering of the chip-birds, like the bursting head
of the uncorked day."

Life Fizz

Let life fizz
from the bottle
running over,
flowing down.

Become a wild
dancing river,
lift the glass,
toast a round.

Taste the giver's
sweet bubbling joy.
Shout thanksgiving,
uncork the day.

Journal Entry for January 5, 1856

"The same law that shapes the earth and stars shapes the snow-flake. Call it rather snow star."

Snow Star

Pines stretch winter gloves,
catch falling flakes, exchange
green gowns for white.

Limbed arms in a winter coat
bow before a pale glass sky.
All is new, a gift,

Looking through the snow
its mesmerizing beauty,
lace curtains hung over day.

How many flakes
fill the sky with white stars?
Do they equal grains of sand?
Ask Abraham's children, or

become a child,
count the crystals, and
marvel as galaxies turn.
Feel eternity fall on your face.

Journal Entry for October 15, 1858

"There is an honest, heartfelt melody. Shall not the voice of man express as much content as the note of a bird?"

Wings

Birds know more of the divine,
are not afraid to dart and sing,
search earth for gifts to bring
children on high branches,
to frolic in the wind.

Perhaps one day all will have wings,
discover the secret of birds,
learn how to fly and sing,
paint the sky with outspread dreams,
connect the dots cloud to cloud.

"My profession is to be always on the alert, to find God in nature, to know his lurking-places, to attend all the oratorios, the operas in nature."

Lurking Places

Divine Spirit, open my eyes
to find you under leaf and mold.
Let me not pass quickly by
and miss your oratorio.

Let opera singers sing the day
through trees, briars, mud and clay
while squirrels squabble in the trees
oblivious, ignoring me.

Let woods buzz with honey bees,
bird chorus fill the skies.
Spirit, do not hide from me,
sing nature's oratorio.

I would not miss the harmony,
should summer season change,
but go from leafy violins,
to whispering winter snow.

Pound kettle drums from above,
paint daises on meadow floors,
let orchestras of morning doves
sing your oratorio.

Open my eyes, Spirit Divine,
guide me to a chambered place,
filled with nature's morning grace,
the music of your oratorio.

Gene G. Bradbury

THE POET'S HOUR

Journal Entry for February 26, 1841

"The good book helps the sunshine in my chamber."

In My Chamber

Steam from my cup
sends smoke signals
into first morning light.

Through windowpanes
flecks of sunshine dot
the pages of my book.

A perfect moment,
holiness in time, to breathe
the aroma of being alone.

Journal Entry for June 24, 1852

"Clouds are among the most glorious objects in nature.
A sky without clouds is a meadow without flowers,
a sea without sails. Some days we have the mackerel fleet."

Paper Sky

Empty pages lay before me,
poised, ready, blank, they cry,
"Bring me song, bring me story."

Fill heavens with sailing ships,
send visitors from other lands,
spreading out in cumulous bands.

I'll write of spring, flowers glorious,
pirates clinging to yardarm sails,
cloud covered poppies on blue hills.

On a voluminous cloudy day
carnival shapes will float on by
write their words on paper sky.

Journal Entry for January 26, 1853

"It is the poet's hour. Mornings when men are new born, men who have the seeds of life in them."

Poet's Hour

Taste and smell
summer night's gloaming,
the strawberry sweetness
of garden fresh flowers.

Sleep in dull hours,
wake in bright daylight,
eyes to the morning,
'tis the poet's hour.

I'll wake to the newness
of the day's dawning light,
take hold of the freshness
a gift from the night.

Journal Entry for June 16, 1852

"Do not the stars, too, show their light for love,
like the fire-flies?"

Stardust

I choose to believe
stardust covers all we know,
settles hope on us below,
to live in starlight's afterglow.

Particles fall, soon neglected,
blown by winds out to sea,
leaving traces on the mantle
where memories used to be.

Give me wakeful eyes to see
invisible stardust all around
sparkling hope in dark places
fire-flies in glowing gowns.

Journal Entry for June 19, 1860

"Something like the woodland sounds will be heard
to echo through the leaves of a good book."

Listen

Turn the pages of a book,
hear wild horses gallop by,
teapots sing in the kitchen,
hens scratch barnyard rye,
motors run, runners flee,
crowds talk, skiers ski,
fields laugh, crickets sing,
woods are chanting,
echoing.

Entry for March 25, 1842

"It is enough if I please myself with writing;
I am then sure of an audience."

Writing

To write,
begin with clear sky . . .

watch chickadees
print Chinese letters
on newly fallen snow,

a pianist
tap dance across
polished keys,

let cloud-shadows
travel silently
over the empty page.

From Familiar Letters

"Blessed is the man who can have his library at hand, and oft pursue the books, without the fear of a taskmaster!"

The Library

The book opens
like a bird in hand
ready to sing.

It may bring tears or
bubbling laughter as I
fall into the arms of words.

Anger may rise,
like bile in the night,
a taste of printed disgust,

or turn to warm tenderness
as soft lamplight falls
over the wings of pages.

From A Yankee in Canada, Excursions

"Even the elephant carries but a small trunk on his journeys."

Traveling Light

Creatures travel light,
elephant trunks,
turtle shells,
and we . . .

fill closets,
storage sheds,
cars and boats,
and . . .

ourselves with fast-food,
visions of platinum t.v.
I no longer know
how to stop the frenzy,
consumed with guilt.

Will my children know
how to pack lightly
like the buffalo?

Journal Entry for December 23, 1851

"It is a record of the mellow and ripe moments that I would keep. I would not preserve the husk of life, but the kernel."

Ripe Moments

Ripe moments, life's seed
seen with open searching eyes,
leaf mold, drifting pollen.

There must be waiting,
time to take a silent breath,
still as a heron on the water,
watching alone in quietness.

Seize now the slippery morsel,
floating lights swimming by,
sunset colors over water,
magic moment, evening sky.

Journal Entry for January 23, 1858

"I cannot conceive of any life which deserves the name,
unless there is in it a certain tender relation to nature."

There is a Place

There is a place I know well
among the meadow flowers.
I go there often in my dreams
and lie down in the grass
to whisper to the daises
the things I'd like to ask.

They nod their heads as if to say,
"These things we've heard before
from travelers who pass us by
and tell of all they hear, and
so we learn standing still
the things that others know."

"O dreamer, pass this way again,
for daises seldom move, unless
a summer wind blows through
to let our petals fly, and so
we await the morning news
from those who pass us by."

GENE G. BRADBURY writes from his home in the Pacific Northwest where he lives with his wife, Debbie. His writing encompasses poetry, short stories, children's stories and education material for adults.

His work may be found in various children's magazines and adult periodicals. Gene teaches adult classes in theology in his area.

Gene has a B.A. in Philosophy, an M.Div., and a Master's Degree in Spiritual Direction. He is involved in numerous writers' workshops and enjoys sharing his stories during school visits.

Visit the writer's blog: scribblinglife.com

Other Books by the Author

Faces From a Broken Star
Short Stories by Gene G. Bradbury
There was a time when traveling across country one might pull into any small town in America and find a mom and pop café. It was a good place to order a fried chicken dinner. Farmers gathered there to compare crop prices and check the weather before working in the field. The local café has disappeared. In these stories you're invited to meet the regulars at the Broken Star Café. Some of the characters may sound familiar. Others who will make you laugh and cry.

Poetry

Traveling in Company
is the first book of poetry by author Gene G. Bradbury.

Quiet Places, Morning Walks: Notes Between Secular and
Sacred is his second book of poetry.

Children's Books by the Author

The Mouse with Wheels in His Head
Fergus dreams of being the first mouse to ride the first Ferris Wheel at the 1893 World's Fair. But how is it to be done?

The Mouse Who Wanted to Fly
Fergus's second adventure takes him to Kitty Hawk where two brothers are going to fly the first airplane.
Should a mouse be on the first flight? Fergus thinks so.

Mischievous Max, A Teddy Bear Story
Max Bear is not a cuddly Teddy Bear. His eyes are beastly and his fur is scratchy. No wonder Leon doesn't want to sleep with him. What if Leon takes Max to bed for just one night? Does he know Max Bear likes to do mischief in the night?

Fergus of Lighthouse Island
This Fergus is named after a great uncle who loved adventure. You may have met him as he rode the first Ferris Wheel and flew with the Wright Brothers at Kitty Hawk. But this Fergus isn't brave at all. He's not looking for adventure. But when a hurricane threatens Lighthouse Island, adventure finds him.

Cloud Climber (An Adventure for Seven to Ten Year Olds)
When Seth and Emily spend a few weeks with their grandparents, they're sure it will be the most boring weeks of their lives. But there is no time to be bored after discovering Three Friends Hill, the Banshee's Cave, and a treasure found in the hayloft of the old barn.

All books available at Amazon.com
or the author's website: genegbradbury.com

BookWilde Children's Books

Visit the author's website:
genegbradbury.com